Level 2

The Nature Kid's Guide to DONKEYS

DAVID ANDERSON

LP Media Inc. Publishing
Text copyright © 2026 by LP Media Inc.
All rights reserved.

For information address LP Media Inc. Publishing,
30012 Variolite St NW, Princeton MN 55371
www.lpmedia.org

Publication Data

Donkeys
The Nature Kid's Guide to Donkeys — First edition.

Summary: "Learn all about Donkeys, the Nature Kid Way"
— Provided by publisher.

ISBN: 979-8-89818-255-7

[1. Donkeys – Non-Fiction] I. Title.

Title: The Nature Kid's Guide to Donkeys

CONTENTS

DONKEY DIGS

People have kept donkeys as farm helpers for over 5,000 years — longer than horses!

Clip-clop! A donkey walks across the sunny farm yard.

Donkeys live on farms all over the world. They share the land with cows, goats, and chickens. Every donkey needs a safe pen, clean water, and a friend to keep it company.

Farmers care for their donkeys each day. They brush their coats and check their hooves for stones. A happy donkey wags its tail and comes running when it sees its owner.

At night, the donkey sleeps in a warm barn. It likes a dry, soft bed of straw. Farm life keeps a donkey healthy, safe, and content.

DESERT DAYS

There are fewer than 600 African wild donkeys left on Earth — they are critically **endangered**!

Whoosh! A wild donkey races across the hot desert sand.

Deep in the hot deserts of northeast Africa lives one of the rarest animals on Earth — the African wild donkey. Temperatures reach 120 degrees, but these tough animals find food where few others can survive.

African wild donkeys drink very little water. They eat dry grass and thorny plants that other animals ignore. The blazing desert sun does not stop them.

About 5,000 years ago, people began taming African wild donkeys and putting them to work. Every donkey alive today is a descendant of those same desert survivors. That toughness never went away.

SIZE UP

The very smallest donkey is the Miniature Mediterranean Donkey. They are only 24-36 inches tall!

Thump! A big donkey stamps its hoof on the dusty ground.

Donkeys come in many sizes. Some are tiny, even when they are full grown. Others can stand over five feet tall — almost as big as a horse!

The biggest donkeys can weigh up to 1,000 pounds. A small one may weigh just 200 pounds. Size depends on the **breed** and where the donkey lives.

Next to a horse, most donkeys look short. But do not let their small legs fool you! Donkeys are very strong for their size and can carry heavy loads all day long.

BIG EARS

DID YOU KNOW?
A donkey's teeth never stop growing throughout its whole life!

Flick! A donkey turns its long ears toward a sound.

A donkey's ears are big and long. They can be 13 inches long! Each ear turns on its own, so a donkey can listen in two directions at once. Those amazing ears catch sounds from far away.

Donkeys have tough hooves that do not need shoes. Their legs are thin but strong. A thick coat keeps them warm in winter and sheds to keep them cool in summer.

Most donkeys are gray or brown. Many have a dark stripe down their back. Some also have a stripe across their shoulders, forming a cross shape.

SUPER SENSES

Sniff! A donkey catches a new smell on the breeze.

Donkeys have amazing senses. Their big ears can hear sounds from very far away. This helps them stay safe from danger long before it gets close.

A donkey has a great nose too. It can smell water from miles away! In the wild, this skill saved their lives in the dry desert.

Donkeys also see very well. They can see almost all the way around them without turning their heads. At night, their eyes work well in the dark. Those big eyes help a donkey spot trouble fast.

MANY KINDS

There are more than 40 million donkeys around the world — that is more than the number of people in California!

14

Whomp! A big donkey bumps its nose against a tiny one.

Donkeys come in many breeds. Miniature donkeys are very small and sweet. They stand only about three feet tall, and kids love to pet them.

Mammoth donkeys are the biggest breed. They are as big as a horse, with long legs and a thick body. Some weigh over 1,000 pounds!

Poitou donkeys have long, shaggy hair that hangs in thick curls. Other breeds have smooth, short coats. Each breed is special in its own way, from tiny to giant.

MUNCH TIME
DID YOU KNOW?
Donkeys can eat prickly thistles and thorny bushes that most other farm animals refuse to touch!
16

Crunch! A donkey bites down on a thick clump of dry hay.

Donkeys eat mostly grass and hay. They munch on food for many hours each day. Their strong teeth chew tough plants with ease.

A donkey also likes straw and bark. Some enjoy a carrot or apple as a treat. But too many treats can make them sick, so farmers give them out sparingly.

Donkeys do not need as much food as horses. Their bodies get more energy from less food. Clean water and dry grass can keep a donkey going strong for miles and miles.

HELPING HANDS

Cleopatra, the famous Egyptian queen, bathed in donkey milk to keep her skin soft!

Swish! A donkey flicks its tail and walks to the barn.

Donkeys give people many things. In some places, people drink donkey milk. It is very creamy and good for your skin.

Donkey hair can be used to make warm cloth. Their soft coats are spun into yarn, which makes cozy blankets and socks.

Donkeys also help the land. Their droppings make the soil rich, helping flowers and food plants grow tall. Donkeys give us more than we might think!

LOUD BRAYS

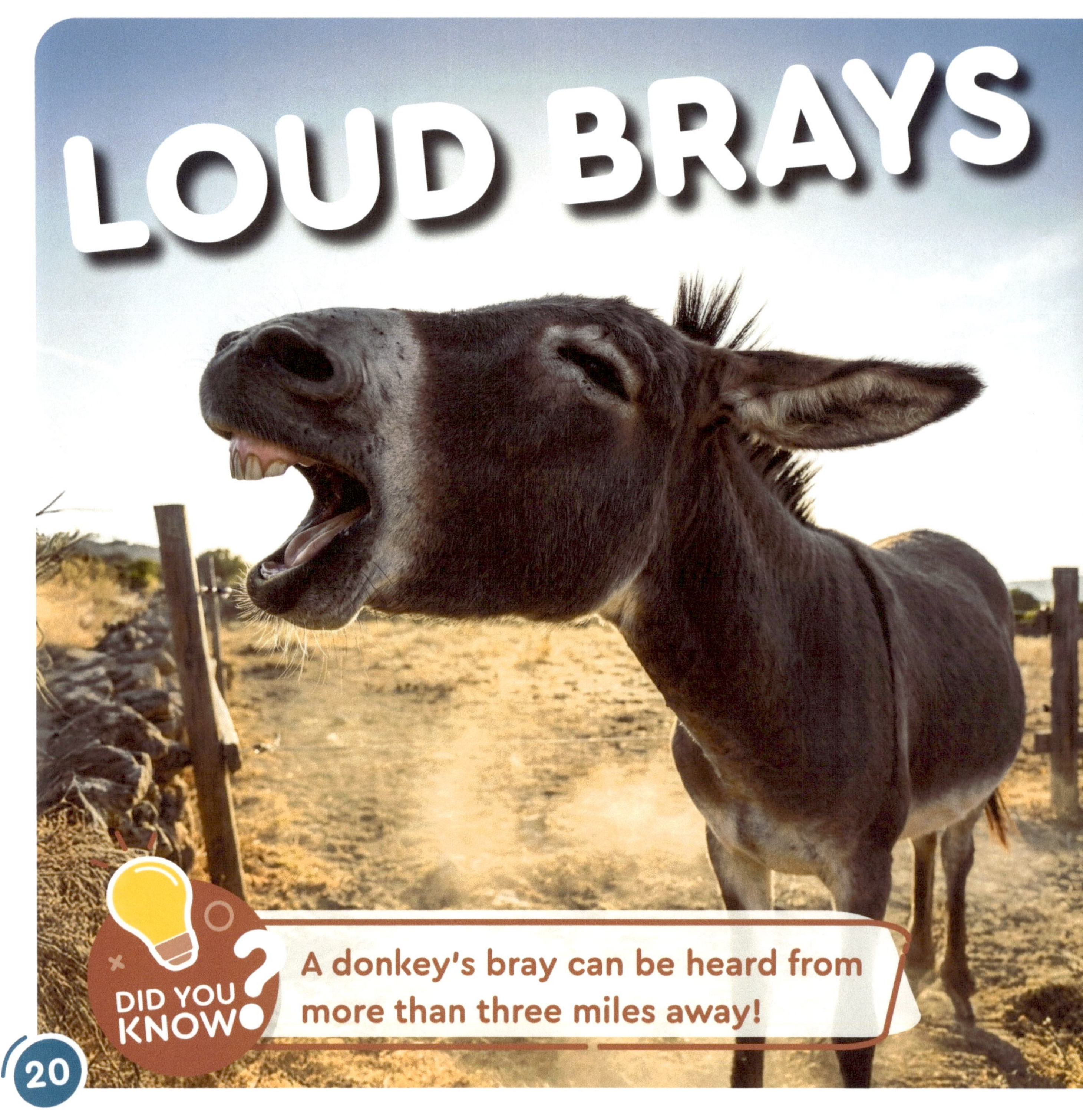

DID YOU KNOW?
A donkey's bray can be heard from more than three miles away!

Hee-haw! A donkey lets out a loud call across the field.

A donkey's loud voice is called a **bray**. It sounds like hee-haw! You can hear it from very far away — it is one of the loudest farm sounds.

Donkeys bray to say many things. A hungry donkey brays for food. A lonely one brays for a friend. They also bray to warn others of danger.

Donkeys talk with their bodies too. Flat ears mean they want space. Ears up mean they feel happy and curious. A slow tail swish shows they are calm and relaxed.

DAY JOBS

FUN
FACT!
Donkeys are most active in the
early morning and late evening
when the air is cool.

Creak! The barn door opens and a donkey peeks outside.

A donkey starts its day at sunrise. It walks out to the field to eat. Grass is the first meal of the day.

After eating, the donkey rests in the shade. It may nap standing up! Donkeys like to take short naps all through the day instead of sleeping all at once.

As the sun sets, the donkey heads back to the barn. It drinks water and eats hay, then settles in for the night. A donkey sleeps only about three hours total — that's much less sleep than a human needs!

TROT ALONG
DID YOU KNOW?
Donkeys place each hoof carefully, one at a time, testing the ground before putting their weight down.
24

Clack! A donkey picks its way down a steep rocky trail.

Donkeys can walk, trot, and run. Most donkeys prefer a slow, steady walk. They do not like to rush anywhere.

A donkey is very steady on its feet. It can walk on rocky ground without slipping, which is why people ride them on steep mountain paths. At the Grand Canyon, donkeys carry visitors down narrow trails!

Donkeys are not as fast as horses. But they can keep going for a long time without getting tired. Their hard hooves grip the ground on even the roughest trails.

DUST BATHS

26

Poof! A donkey drops down and rolls in a patch of dirt.

Donkeys love dust baths! They drop to the ground and roll back and forth. The dust covers their body from head to hoof.

Rolling in dust is not just fun. It helps keep bugs and flies away. The dry dirt also keeps their coat clean and healthy.

A donkey picks the same dusty spot each time. After a good roll, it stands up and shakes off. A cloud of dust flies into the air! Then the donkey walks off, feeling great and bug-free.

HERD LIFE

FUN FACT!
A donkey can remember another donkey
it has not seen in 25 years — that is a
longer memory than most people have!

Stomp! A donkey trots over to its friends near the creek.

Donkeys are social animals. They like to live in groups called herds. A herd can have just a few donkeys or many.

Each herd has a leader. The leader is usually a strong female called a **jenny**. She picks where the herd goes and when they rest.

Donkeys groom each other to stay close. They nibble at each other's necks and backs, which helps build trust. A donkey with no friends can feel sad and lonely, so farmers try to keep at least two together.

NEW LIFE

FUN FACT!
When a male donkey and a female horse have a baby, it is called a mule!

30

Nicker! A mother donkey nuzzles her new baby foal.

A mother donkey carries her baby for about 12 months, almost a full year! The baby is born right on the ground, usually at night when it is quiet.

The father is called a **jack**. He is bigger and louder than the mother. The mother is called a jenny, and she does most of the work raising the baby.

Most jennies have just one baby at a time. Twins are very rare. A new foal can stand up in under an hour and starts walking soon after!

FUZZY FOALS

DID YOU KNOW?
A baby donkey's legs are almost as long as an adult's legs — they just need to grow into them!

Pitter-pat! A baby donkey wobbles on its brand new legs.

Baby donkeys are called foals. They are born with soft, fuzzy fur. Their legs are long and wobbly at first.

A foal drinks its mother's milk right away. It stays close to her side for warmth and food. The foal nurses many times each day.

Foals love to play! They run and kick and jump around the field. By six months, they start to eat grass. As they grow, their fuzzy coat turns smooth and sleek.

MOM KNOWS

A jenny can tell her own foal apart from dozens of others just by its smell!

Snort! A mother donkey gently nudges her foal.

A jenny is a loving mom. She stays by her foal day and night, keeping it safe at all times.

The jenny teaches her baby how to eat and drink. She shows it where to find the best grass. She also shows it how to stay with the herd and follow the rules.

If danger comes, the jenny acts fast. She stands between the threat and her foal. She will kick or bite to keep her baby safe. A jenny is fierce, brave, and always ready to protect her little one.

WORK HARD

In some mountain villages, donkeys carry mail, medicine, and supplies to places no road can reach!

Rumble! A donkey pulls a heavy cart up a steep dirt road.

Donkeys have helped people work for thousands of years. They carry heavy bags of food and water. They pull carts down dusty roads and up steep hills.

In many places, donkeys do this work every day. They walk long trails through hills and valleys. People count on them when trucks and cars cannot go.

Donkeys are very patient. They do not give up when the work is hard. Rain or shine, they keep going. That is why people all over the world love and depend on them.

BEST BUDS

Donkeys sometimes adopt baby animals like lambs and goat kids, protecting them as their own!

Snuffle! A donkey rubs its nose against a horse friend's neck.

Donkeys make great friends with other farm animals. They bond with horses, goats, and sheep. A donkey can even be best friends with a cat or dog!

Farm animals feel safe with a donkey nearby. Cows and sheep stay calm around them. Many farmers keep a donkey in the pasture just to guard the other animals from coyotes.

Donkeys also enjoy being around people. They come close when they want to play. A happy donkey will follow you around like a puppy, hoping for a scratch behind those big ears!

GLOSSARY

bray
The loud hee-haw sound a donkey makes

breed
A specific kind of donkey or other animal

jenny
A female donkey

jack
A male donkey

endangered
When a type of animal has so few left that it could disappear forever